Whatever
The Name

Pierre Lepori

Translated from the Italian by Peter Valente

SPUYTEN DUYVIL
New York City

Publication of this volume is in part made possible by
ProHelvetia, the Swiss Arts Council.

prohelvetia

Pierre Lepori: QUALUNQUE SIA IL NOME.

© Edizioni Casagrande SA, Bellinzona, 2003
Translation © 2017 Peter Valente

ISBN 978-1-944682-34-7

Library of Congress Cataloging in Publication Data applied for.

WHATEVER THE NAME

CONSCIOUSNESS OF THE TRUTH
Fabio Pusterla

Pierre Lepori is a young author, but not very young[1], who has long been working quietly and diligently to achieve his own voice, now exactly defined in the poems collected in this large volume.

The caution and the wait however, should not only be regarded as signs of a fruitful literary apprenticeship, during which the poetic word of this highly cultivated intellectual has tried to get rid of the reference models too obvious or too bulky. There was also this, of course, and those who were able to follow the development of this work cannot but admire the expressive results which we now know are infrequently achieved: a substantially plain language, with moderate lyrical bursts or metaphorical snapshots and some vein of precious minerals not exhibited too much, at first glance transitive, the controlled pace; torn, and strengthened, by the power of images and the burning quick connections, which lift the reader into a very large dimension, poised between a dream-like atmosphere (mostly incubates who dream) and the shadows of lost archetypes, history lived on their skin, suffering and throbbing behind each verse, and significant chorus, allegorical. With just a few strokes to seemingly paint the narrative and describe with bruised color the timeless tragedy:

Henceforth what was known as rain, was now salt,

the smoke rising from the sleepy village, known as chimney-smoke,

---

1 Pierre Lepori, was born in Lugano, Switzerland in 1968. He would have been 34 years old when the book was published in 2003. A year later Lepori won the Swiss Schiller prize for Poetry (the highest award for a Swiss author) for *Whatever the Name*.

was in fact the cause of my despair. White bread,

clothes carefully tucked away in the closets

for the summer months, the mothballs thrown in the sand.

Everything was given to us

once and for all.

Yet another aspect, even more intimately connected to the very root of this poem, can be seen is an account of the long journey of the book: writing, for Lepori, is only secondarily an aesthetic operation, because he knows that naming things, whatever the name, assumes the conscious responsibility of making them into a line of confrontation, to confess the unbearable cruelty and to recognize its enormous weight. This is poetry as a gesture of the body and the mind, and how difficult the choice, then: no ornament or relief, but mediated revolt. Some years ago, accompanying the first poetic apparitions of Pierre Lepori (in the seventh issue of the important *Journal on Contemporary Italian Poetry*, published in Milan, by Marcos and Marcos, 2001), Franco Buffoni already called attention to this aspect of the work, precisely observing that the author had, "waited long (though he was always writing poetry) before accepting himself as a poet, and deciding to come out." Now we can better measure the deeper significance of such a statement; it is precisely the will to "come out" which is the thread that sews and unifies the two great parts of the book, and the numerous micro-sections, of the work.

The terrible hiding place, from which comes this bold word, is revealed in the entire courageous first part of the collection, whose journey to an outlet of conscience and a voice, is already suggested by the two epigraphs: it goes from the strangled silence "when the worst was over" to the difficult but inevitable choice of giving each thing a name: "Now everything / is given its name / without exception, / whatever the name." There in the middle, in the years and centuries of bourgeois drama, there is the guilty silence, the omission, and the deception that all combine in a single mute destiny of generations: "because each generation is a deadbolt." Regions of cold light and false peace, a place of duties and lies, bristling with rocks and sticks and predators: "Oddly, peace has preserved / the feline eyes of hate. The voice of the vulture." Everything is quiet, nothing ominous can happen: "All the houses have gardens / and in those gardens, children."; everything is perfectly normal: "The silence / is exhausted by the attempt to keep silent. / The table has been prepared with skill / but this is not enough, / a shadow falls each time the child laughs." And being in this segregated world of dignified suffering and anesthesia, and under constant pressure, "Damned to be unable to recognize the opposition.": the vine grows in the absence of walls, pretending the wall is not there, it disguises the absence; the "light diversion," the "unspoken affection" produce ruin, a "bloom of ashes."

Poetry, affirmed by the author in the concluding note, certainly cannot save or redeem; it can lead: lead forward, toward the ability to say that which has not been said for a long time, shaking it off like a hair shirt; but also to go back, giving a voice to, if not a meaning, to the silence that has elapsed. In fact it's a desperate attempt but a victorious one, deployed by Pierre Lepori, using a special technique: it is not to tell of private secrets, to build an autobiography in verse; instead it is to investigate the deep links that have crystallized over time, transferring the biography of an almost mythical screen, translating a narrative report almost impossible in psychoanalysis. The reader cannot, and should not, try to turn the elements of the drama into a finished story: what's left of that history are absolute emblems, primary materials, such as water and fire, the Mother and the Father, the rock and the cry. Sometimes, in certain texts, the daily tangible reality will seem to take the upper hand, as happens in the mirror-images of "Morning" and "Evening," and again in "The end of the journey" : but this turn into a miserable backdrop, is only to denounce the failure of that reality, which is immediately snatched up by a very ancient restlessness, enigmatic and disturbing. More often, however, the landscape and environments are located in another place, with unrecognizable family interiors, anonymous valleys, mountains, fog, rocks, and turbid rivers. And children, especially children: crushed by the weight of what is incomprehensible because unnamed, and thus intractable. It's no wonder the first part of the book ends in the gamble of an illustrious remake[2], which leads to the implosion of Rimbaud, with "Seven Year Old Poets": thematizing, once again, the central link between poetry and constriction, between the need to write and the condition of solitary asphyxiation. "My torment / is when / I do not believe / in harmony," wrote Ungaretti; indeed, this is a poetry of pure torment.

The call to Ungaretti is less peregrine than it seems, if we look at the concluding section of the collection, with the challenging title, "Brothers II (The Meaning of Battle)," as a the flipside to the celebrated attack in "Happiness": "Of what regiment are you / brothers ?," which in Lepori becomes a statement of defiance and a proposal of collective identification:

What's different
about us,
brothers?

But the brotherhood of Ungaretti entailed the abolition of an apparent difference (one caused by war) in the name of a more pro-found common humanity, hidden under the mask of the uniforms; to Lepori, analogous and contrary, it arises from the full acceptance of a diversity that breaks the yoke of fake normalizing equality.

The the second part of *Whatever the Name*, in fact, significantly titled "Brothers," is, in the words of the author, "an attempt to make political the expulsion from the pain of the unsaid." And the attempt must arrive right at this point, in the "we" still unformed, still only hoped for or invoked, which has already, however, exceeded the in-dividual solitude, the personal silence : "the regiment of the deniers / takes over the voice of the parade / But the masks, oh what masks, / they are sewn right into the skin. " From the ego to recognition of an "us", to the "first 'we' raised": here is the direction that the author has tried stubbornly to follow and make clear in the work. So, if the first

---

2 I re-draw the body in words, // the few that I have left.

poem in "Brothers" is still "tending to the silence / between the half-closed shutters," recording the last echoes of a drama and not a shared secret, the concluding lines open up to something that looks like a proclamation, enunciated under those same windows that protect the "torturers of the silent":

There is only exile from yourself
and a private pain is a minor thing.
Alone, crying inside, is not
screaming along with everyone.

But if life has any meaning
then marching with anger beneath the windows
and with contempt for the past
is a way of saying
"We", "We, Everyone."

Not a ransom, not a useless poetic revenge; a judgment, however, as suggested by the Pavese verses chosen as a compass for the second part of the book, ie a shift from private pain to the political horizon, which seals the volume by opening up to a vision of the future, an assumption of dignified survival. Not just for those who departed from the "nights [that] followed one another," open wide like a cramp in the prefatory poem; this is no small event for the reader, who Pierre Lepori has led by the hand through the book's secular hells and purgatory, lit only by the will to speak, to point out the evil so as to be able to defeat it. *The* evil? Of course, their own evil; ie the silence, the mask, the submission.

Do not issue from our mouth,
word that sows the dragon.
It is true, the air is heavy,
the light foaming with acids and enzymes
and on the black swamp it weighs the veil of mosquitos.

Ingeborg Bachmann

And when the worst was over
a great silence was formed
like a still lake
over a submerged city.
(…)
Now everything
is given its name
without exception,
whatever the name
I must give it to her.

Margherita Guidacci

1. DIALOGUE[3]

The nights followed one another,

the tables previously full, the feast now deserted,

the sluggish hours of the pre-Dawn light among the chestnut trees,

and lights on the distant snow.

But it will come, later,

you said, the frozen days in the light of the sun. Afterwards,

songs strangely out of tune, songs of peace, the eyes blinded but finally

at rest.

But this is still deceptive

like a persistent loud barking within the silence.

Oddly, peace has preserved

the feline eyes of hate. The voice of the vulture.

---

3 In the following "dialogue" (starting on page 12 and concluding on page 30) some parts of the text are aligned on the right; this is equivalent to the mother's / ancestor's voice. The dialogue is structured precisely on this alternation of the author's voice (here rendered as "you") and "their voice" (on the right).

Sharp pains, splintered words,

like weeds in the grass.

Again without rest

until the blank page is filled: each new beginning

you count on the palm of the hand,

is a new vigil, with one eye open,

a cry without echo.

It is not true that you have finished looking.

There is something that slowly destroys the comfort zone

of your recognizable fears. But to able to exist is already

one step you haven't taken. Slowly,

very slowly, the evil is suffered and paid for.

Even fewer are those that recognize the One that exists.

And in this deafness the body has chosen,

you set out to prove

that you are not mute! Indeed, a flourish

of gestures. A flower

in a heap of stones, dormant and frail

in the cold sunlight.

The heap of stones is a garden of stone,

stone flowers and sky above.

But the Mother cleansed of all sins

raises her arms toward the horizon, moaning,

and goes back to being a daughter.

Suddenly in her bowels a tremor:

an angel has fallen, the silvered wings

and beaks of a bird of prey in the white sun.

She remembers then: there was no garden, and she

endured the punishment of being alive,

closed off and lost while waiting

for the father a face,

between receiving beatings with a stick, like with the stones,

in some filthy corner of the backyard. Your father's not coming,

and America is far away, there are poisonous spiders

and scorpions. All the houses have gardens

and in those gardens, children.

Why search among the dead? Everything shatters against

that nature which made you an orphan, because only the son

can produce a child. And this is not granted to her.

Offended or seized by laughter,

how many words are necessary to give voice to the silence?

Aren't you perhaps the ambiguous one,

wounded by daring gestures,

so different from their ambitious

declarations of love.

But dig, then, dig,

ferrit, pet, spider

mole.

Because everything is now offered to you

like an array of sparkling lights. Again there is a train

and the blue and white shop sign in the early morning. Where is this?

In the dream the dream in the forest

of words. And if you hear the voices

speaking, listen. Things

continue to exist,

to halt the moment

in its weary eyed race

to final damnation.

And you shouted, for once, only once, like an animal,

nothing more than an ugly beast.

        (Now stop shouting!

        Something has changed

        Is anyone here?)

No one. And the barren plain flows beyond the window

of a useless solitary search.

But the countryside is not liquefied

from your passage or your gaze,

you haven't sufficiently comforted

that pale sky.

And now? In what direction

should you go? In the beginning

there was at least the forest, that turn

toward something that was named, the flesh wasn't hidden.

Now

it's like a meadow filled with weeds in the throes of a foaming hot sun,

the light of death that mocking sound in the silence. And there is an ache

as if it were the dawn after a forced march at night,

and it's like a pain with a moderate voltage,

lasting a long time, and unexpected,

and no thought – at all – to cultivate

any voice in the desert.

The horizon is empty now.

No one will come: after the explosion there followed the great silence

and the sons passed by, moaning like dogs, now they are gone,

they live their lives

with pride.

(Instead, how we suffered, with the harsh beatings from the stick

and the long days with those who bent our backs.

But by the fire, we said, we will have children like olives.[4]

---

4   This is a reference to Psalm 128: "filii tui sicut stories olivarum in circuitu mensae tuae" (Thy children like the olive branches: round about thy table)

They never stopped violating you,

infecting you. Now there is no light in the tunnel,

it narrows the gut around your waist.

      (Pretend you're on a journey, your equipment the adjectives,

           and on the wooden staircase leading to the bedroom

                      say

              "our suffering means nothing."

        Do not lie, so as to be able to commerce with these ghosts

                that still turn your back.

                What things are you writing?)

2. MORNING

From the window

a line of windows as a backdrop

and a sunbeam.

The square is deserted at this hour –

it the reign of the stray cat;

he tries to warm up for a moment – before the day inundates

the austere avenue – rummages the warmth hidden in the leaves

bows to the sleeping gardens, the vast trees adorning

the eyelash of the street.

The sky that becomes smooth and turquoise

seems to wait motionless

inside this blue hour – in the open sunbeam of the dawn.

An old woman turned and without sadness,

left her door ajar and came out onto the street with her dog,

a filthy indefinable hound with a purple snout

that pulled on the collar and yanked it.

But a first shutter has opened —now the distribution of newspapers —

and when the light fog invades, with the stagnant winter,

there is a red glow, here is a young man

and here is an old man, each with a dog and collar

and someone who whistles clearing his throat a bit too much

on the road to the hospital.

Now a rhythmic step on the stairs,

a beautiful woman in heels

and she is made up so plainly

that no one even hears

the jingling as she takes out

a bundle of silver keys.

Everything is normal, as the night goes belly up.

A view through the window

the cars that dare with their attention straight ahead

and discretely swarming,

and others prepare their taxes and open the rolladen shutters,

pipes gurgling,

the milk foaming,

and on the table's plastic covering the mother

prepares six dishes.

3. Eyes Shut

A child without a childhood.

Solitude complicit.

A gulf between existing and knowing.

Someone has to pay, one day

and then they lay headfirst on top of their children.

It's a question of justice.

The fates like concentric circles.

And you must call it duty, you must call it silent death.

There was no garden, only houses. She endured

the punishment of being alive, the punishment of existence

with the beatings received with a stick, the clatter of stones,

in some filthy corner.

Voiceless between gritted teeth,

sometimes, but only at the end of her rope, exhausted,

she clambered up onto the toilet seat

and from there she looked out from the narrow space

that overlooked the courtyard;

outside the slow and unconscious summer.

The days were rough

the shop and the washtub for the mothers

and a fine detachment for the fathers.

A white panama hat,

and travel overseas;

and the well-known secret the unspeakable

sin. How to tell the children

how to say it to the children's children.

Snow and silence.

The silence

is exhausted by the attempt to keep silent.

The table has been prepared with skill

but this is not enough,

a shadow falls each time the child laughs.

The bastard son

of words.

Your son, your father,

who are they and why?

"Suicide," only a word,

no one any longer has that desire,

there is no time for remorse,

because his guilty life is a fragile thing.

The children are the bread of the dark womb.

But existence prevents us from existing,

the full day drains us,

distances us further from each other. The silence

of peace slowly gangrenous up to the claw, the bite

and the tearing, the jugular vein ripped out.

(the work of the day is complete:

epileptic roots charred, are asleep.)

Sleep.

And nothing else.

No dreams, only tossing and sweating

in a bed of duties and fees to be paid, until the volcanic dawn rises.

(I lost my child.

It's not important.)

From then on the house was white. Soaking wet under the winter sun

and the shadows of the elder tree. The unchanging

sky was clear for days to come,

the scars healed,

the sweat dried.

Henceforth what was known as rain, was now salt,

the smoke rising from the sleepy village, known as chimney-smoke,

was in fact the cause of my despair. White bread,

clothes carefully tucked away in the closets

for the summer months, the mothballs thrown in the sand.

Everything was given to us

once and for all.

But the cry that arose from the stomach

would never give birth to speech.

The roads could be drenched with rain and the white snow coat

yet another steep lawn descending into the valley.

The raven could appear magnified on the branch, with a word of disgrace,

but no one would notice. The fog with its odors would be

reassuring like milk

in a blue plastic bucket.

4. Night

The light is out: tonight, all

the cats are gray, the guard rail reflects

the headlights that the most prudent of drivers turn on low.

There is no fog,

only a light curtain of gaseous fumes from the exhaust pipes below,

the air is clear, but it seems as though something braked in order to look

and advances toward the white light, and all of a sudden the air was singed,

cars swerve and you hear the rhomboids of the weary motors driving uphill
toward the traffic lights.

From a shopping bag

sprout a bunch of scallions and the ticket from the large department store
falls to the ground;

the day ends in fits and starts, it's necessary – at first – to shut off the cash
register,

then count the money. The boy

pushes the cart and smiles and it is important to forget that smile.

There is no wind, just this strange premature warmth

in advance of the season, it constricts the blood flow, puts pressure on the
sides of the head

and among the folds of the too full body. The flower girl pours cold water

and then hot water on the sunflowers, sloppily, it's already dark,

it's unclear where the sound of the horns is coming from – there are wounds
with no name –

the puff of air from the crowded bus has an odor and there are human
sounds.

Someone said – during coffee hour – that this morning there was a suicide
from the bridge

and looking through the window she thought that elegant things,

like the arm of the yellow steam shovel that works

in the silence of the interposed window,

sometimes they console: like flowers, a pleasant evening, they console,

the flower girl from Supermarket.

5. Eyes Wide Open

Would like to have poisonous eyes,

invisible like the mouth, without being ashamed of the abyss

so as to swallow a certain gray of the sky

going down headlong toward the entrance to the stomach.

Silence is your heart of wind and your childhood home,

a wet branch invaginated between two valleys, a sad place

where the walls were stained and where there were spurs

and the fields are always desolate, even during the summer.

It's a headache that besieges you

up from the base of the skull and from behind

it's a tightening that freezes. Seek to medicate

this persistent agony;

Yet it's certain that behind this

stiff neck there is a way

of standing on one's own two feet despite the cost

under this hailstorm of memories.

Along the valley you cling

to an idea that is the foundation of your speech,

always unchangeable and willing

to cry out to the gneiss and the lichens.

But when the darkness becomes dense over things

and when the heat of the moment is dampened

you have to keep moving deeper into the abyss

with no one to accompany you, and deeper in the abyss

the mountain is without a name.

Along the valley scattered with tears

in the burning wastes cut off by the earthly river

are the so-called prison houses of the body

and you hate the crags and the concrete covering

that consolidates the sides of the vineyard.

In retribution, you despise nature

but have no other way to descend to Calvary.

They are trapped behind walls of silence,

scraps of dirt and loneliness.

You can't deny it: today it begins,

everything starts with a demand to open, finally,

the book of the dead. Not much light

on the book of the game played at your place.

Rough paper

that a slow fire burns out of this world

without tears.

Yes. Yes.

No. No.

It seems easy, and it's written in the following pages,

but there was a page missing in the book as it was handed down,

like non fertile drips of gall

the truth didn't quench your anger. Parched earth of the fathers

with strong teeth, eyes fixed on the centuries. Perhaps if there was a war

you would have known him from his blood, and though there was violence

you would have found again the dried sperm

on his cheeks.

But it was not because of the shedding of the semen and the blood

that silence became a cruel fact. It only took a light diversion,

an unspoken affection, fire burning at the roots.

So everything that would have bloomed would have been a bloom of ashes.

From now on, even just to know

is punishable with guilt.

And it was the flowering

of the guilty wisteria, the ivy of shame.

A wall that isn't a wall, but the vine pretends there's one.

Substantiated a pure lie, oh child,

how you would have been able to have a voice:

a Door in the milk of the Centuries,

but now only lichens and molds are your mantles,

weep tears of wine.

(It's always raining on the larches and the chestnut trees.

Agony of stone, truce

that preceded the fall:

roots of hatred do not breed children.)

Only occasionally a human voice calling you, you acknowledge it
with a whisper,

and the joy on your face drips like wax,

the world starts to throb and pulsates with the voice and the pain.
And you'll decipher

it tonight, embracing the mirror of a poem,

the duty, without rules, of truth.

But then down, again, headlong,

image after image. There is no rest if the place sought

is Red which is accessed by a door three times barred,

because each generation is a deadbolt,

every angel a fake messenger

its iridescent wings have all the colors of deceit.

One day you hear a black lake as the grunting of a pigsty

and down below – sandstone of memories – a scream of dissonant shades.

From that day on a demon of words pesters you

it pushes you to the bottom, the head inside the aqueous dark.

Shock has plagued the word,

flocks of merciless clouds poison

the heat by now the sky is silent:

there are no human footprints in the marsh,

nor does the ice allow it;

to drain the white

time is needed to count the ages,

for you – the middle generation – there's only

a series of rusty abortions.

Or maybe not, plant a cry

exactly in the center of the maelstrom like a branch

it will be a truce

which you can take with you to the tired Legions of the dark,

the human in them still drags itself

toward the warm regions of the light.

The lukewarm shade in the container of the hand

like the side of you that is aware of the truth.

6. The End Of The Journey

In the night an illuminated window that appears and disappears,

while the wind causes swarming shadows of branches

of a menacing loquaciousness,

a cry is heard from a house very far away,

it is a cry from long ago,

empty beating of shutters.

At each step a crossroads, in the intermittent cold of the headlights,

veering silently under the fabric of the sky,

distant clouds, with the red glow of a reflected city.

And you're still wandering in this wasteland

of bifurcated streets without end,

the clatter of footsteps is a spectrum of sounds,

among the slow-moving cars in the fog

The only companion this white host of winters,

and the damp houses inhabited without noise:

it's clear now, while the night welcomes you,

that time was a slow poison,

that kept quiet about the neglect.

There is a gap at the end of the journey:

a shock on the surface of the mirror,

he goes out again to the city where he remains

silently exhausted.

At every step gravel underneath,

in the mirror he sees every other face, never his own

on this random night, the fear

remains intact and pale as the squad on a ship of ghosts,

it soars to a peak above the destiny of the word,

one final time sorely mocking

this need for pain.

And the day is now a stunned child calling out,

but no one responds.

And in a startled state the night answered:

unborn!

But *you* exist and speak

and look for the warmth that soothes.

How to resist, at night

and survive?

And especially:

when you arrive at the bottom and you're as desperate as before?

FORMS OF WATER

In the haze from the fogbanks,

the superimposed layers –*the dense fog* –

that cleanse the objects inside the whiteness,

the moisture in which peace is found,

there the child walks.

The green becomes greener crossing into the wilderness,

descending to the limit of the forest,

no longer a part of the opaque world,

until lost in the woods,

among the hazel borders

it abandons itself.

But this is a forest, this child, and the leaves

are drenched; the feet interrupt

the sound of the sluggish swamp,

advancing and descending into the darkness of opposites:

where he awaits the fear

the body remembers,

in the center, towards the margin

that knits the web of death,

at the precise point in which it deciphers the futility.

And he is seen walking alone and barefoot.

Look at the candle flame.

First it's blue,

then onto the black wick the gush of yellow wax

incandescent and like certain yellows of Christmas, of

the fireplace in the old house, nocturnal songs being sung:

but the flame burning on a log

is red, its heart is red

and it appeared like a mirage

and it had a sound and a flavor,

gold and pine in the summer night.

But the flames could never be touched

never dissolve the tears

the perfect shadow of the light.

Fire and water, if they are fighting in the whirlpool of the unborn child,

leave him with the tiny claw-like fingers

docked at the edge of life.

A doctor will say, between bright surges of light,

what a narrow escape

but inside the whiteness nobody could hear

the sharp clang of a conviction with no possibility of release.

Damned to be unable to recognize the opposition.

Then there was the sudden release,

the sound of a metal knocker,

the face shorn of any distinctive marks, the dead part

of the face exposed, whichever face,

but the child survived the battle and rests over there,

initially stunned, afraid,

inclined to wandering, but forced to flee,

because he senses the fire and the water,

two animals sniffing around and grunting

and breathing down his neck who would sooner or later capture him.

But he's already caught as by the darkness of a spider's web,

by the voice of the fog, or the water, or the fire.

And the result is a house in black and white,

spinning in the summer and during the winter

where the child, if he ran, is always motionless,

and if he shouts his cries take shape

and petrify.

Of course, there are no words

that will give him back the heat

without the fear of burning;

give him back the breath of milk

without fear of dissolving and perishing.

Of course, looking back, it was right to accuse and to spit,

but on the threshold of the final string of spit

the final stream of blood

there will be no figures to meet

with the name of father and mother

The body is known before them.

The baby always seems to shout, "Hands!" "Body!"

give me back the pain of fire, the orgasm of fear,

where the skin borders another skin!

Sound of distant rain, behind walls of impotence,

an echo of crying though not recognized or sympathized for,

only tucked away in the dark.

The body is a wall

behind which there is silence,

where the arms are immerged,

a dark and indifferent pool,

because if the child calls out and expects an answer,

there is only darkness

the night is long

and it's better not to hope.

The only way to save himself

would come from outside language itself

and from its winter

because it's not possible to go deeper!

The hardest steel

would bend like wax over a flame.

Its mirror

would reflect the black of the wall.

Say that the valley is a wound,

something that one day was divided

and the sun quickly departed on the horizon.

Do not say: the valley is my life,

do not say: fog, rocks, grass, streams

these things are the cause. The seasons

are the harvest of men, and it is the fathers

who are responsible

son.

POSTSCRIPT

At home during the rainy morning

I now gaze tenderly at these objects:

but there are other objects, like those at the end of a dream

that re-emerge frightened and turning

shout, "What was your dream?"

Then for the first time I touch the surface of the glass of water,

and run my fingers along the table, under the clear light.

I want to say, looking back,

without having burned these open hands,

that I see no more than a helpless, unarmed, mass

and the chrysanthemum of the mute.

So go away now, specters and mosquitos!

In my eyes the darkness has withdrawn

with the arrival of the morning.

Only the assassins are still smiling, on the day of oblivion.

While in them silence crouches down

I re-draw the body in words,

                                        the few that I have left.

Seven Year Old Poets[5] —Arthur Rimbaud

for A M.P. Demeny

And the Mother shuts the school notebook filled with assignments

and saunters off, extremely proud and with a self-satisfied air, not noticing

behind her, those clear blue eyes and the fresh scar on the forehead,

unaware of the soul of her child, lost in dreams of filth.

He sweats obedience all day long; he's a bright

an intelligent kid; but with a nervous tick and other obscure signs

that seemed to point to a bitter hypocrisy in his nature.

In dark moldy corridors he rubbed his balls until it hurt, and while
                                                          walking

he stuck out his tongue, and shutting his eyes tight he saw a shower of
                                                          exploding stars.

A door opened onto the evening: by lamplight,

up above, on the roof, you could see him, gasping for air,

under a gash of sunlight.

---

5 At this point Lepori inserted a translation into Italian of Rimbaud's "Les Poets de Sept ans." I have translated Lepori's text. It is an "interpretative translation," as Lepori's is in Italian, of Rimbaud's poem.

Especially during summer, with a vacant look in his eyes, stupefied,

he would lock himself, slamming the door shut, in the cool blue latrines:

there he could think, at peace, his nostrils taking in the familiar odors.

Washed clean of the stink of the day, and behind the house,

in the little patch of garden, in winter moonlight,

squatting at the foot of a wall, buried in sticky clay

and rubbing his eyes so that the visions would come,

he heard the tortured fruit trees trying to spread their leaves.

What a shame! His only friends were these skinny kids,

sickly and with pockmarked faces, hatless, rheumy-eyed punks, with black

and yellowed fingers from smoking cigarettes, disheveled kids that hide

their fists in their shit-stained paints,

speaking to each other with the sweet voices of idiotic angels!

And if she discovered him committing these filthy acts against God,

she was absolutely horrified; the profound tenderness

of the child caused her shame. Good for her!

Those soft blue eyes of hers were a sham!

At the age of seven he wrote novels, about the great desert,

where exiled Freedom shines brightly,

he wrote of magical forests, riverbanks, savannahs, and bright suns!

He pored through glossy magazines, for inspiration,

where he saw plump Spanish and Italian women in erotic poses.

And then a young girl arrived, with dark brown eyes, dressed like an Indian,

and a year older than he, the daughter of workers who lived next door;

she wrestled him into a corner, and climbed on top of him,

and when he was firmly underneath her he bit her ass;

it was easy enough since she never wore panties;

Finally he gave up, beaten by her fists and heels, and dragged his sore bones

back to his room with her bodily odors clinging to him like cheap perfume.

He dreaded those cold Sundays in December,

where he'd have to sit at the large mahogany table, hair slicked back with oil,

reading the pages of the GOOD BOOK, turning the leaves of cabbage!;

Each night it was the same; dreams disturbed his sleep in the alcove.

He doesn't love God; he loves the workers, those strong men

seen on the streets in the wild evening, after work, wearing their dirty jackets, walking back towards the suburbs, past the newsboys

who bang on drums, where there is roaring laughter,

and the shouting of slogans directed against the angry mob.

He dreamed of a sexual meadow, where healthy perfumes,

luminous waves, and gilded puberties,

quietly blend in the alembic and then vanish into the golden air.

He delighted in the darkest things, profoundly,

when, in his blue room with the high ceilings,

the doors shut and the blinds down, the walls damp

from the humidity, he poured over his novel day and night,

the pages opening onto ochre skies and submerged forests,

flowers unfolding into starry flesh,

vertigo, collapse, ruin and then the infinite mercy!

All the while the sounds of the city continued

below – but he was alone, stretched across the unbleached canvas,

with violent premonitions of sails beating against rough winds!

BROTHERS

In these poems the events will take place –if carried out --
not because reality wants it this way,
but because this is what the intelligence has decided.
Individual poems and books of poems aren't to be read as autobiography
but as judgment

Cesare Pavese

The wreck happened without any strong winds,
it was calm but cold, enough
was enough, a long way from the coast, halfway
between one of the corners and a door.

Bartolo Cattafi

1.

We believed snow was white and nobody

saw the halos

of yellow, with the corroded edges.

We tried to hear the silence

between the half-closed shutters and we didn't know

that the sun was already derailed.

2.

Legions of corpses from the house

have started bleating,

clogs beat on the dirty wood floors in the stalls,

noise that was deafening,

they drank while intoxicated and collapsed:

because dissipation is sweet,

everything is absolutely quiet in the flesh,

on the inner face

you have never known.

3.

There wasn't a loud bang:

how come no one has told *him*,

it's like a shout that never ends that's never extinguished,

slipping endlessly on the knife's blade.

The skin is torn open and throbs

but does not yield, intact inside the pain

and more simply (the mothers say)

for the *life of poverty* you took a fall once

like a thief abandoned on the street.

4.

Fragments, brothers,

a broken image that tells us

he kept silent about the

exact cut of the blade

but no less infamous was the shame

of pushing us into the world as prey

and who defended

the predator.

5.

The wind is forceful now and the water greasy and cold rain

cruelly beats against the window.

How many times

under the heavy vapors, in the streets,

or in the heat of the room:

watching in the dark. A rain that doesn't weep

but heat that collects in your hands,

opaque.

6.

So, despite the fact that we wanted

to embrace under the threat of stones and abuse,

there was someone who said: "Incest"

and so full of love for us

for our bluish wrists

that he tightened the rope and rubbed out the name

until what remained

was just an empty word, "brothers."

Exactly like everyone else

like the generations that preceded us

in the illusion that denied non-love

could be a kind of love.

7.

No choice but to be born

in the form of the father,

yet mute anger and faceless agony

became like a sword.

And because of the silence he wrecked himself

the weaker ones were overwhelmed and fell

while the others will only end up hating each other

because the name 'brothers' was misunderstood,

torturers of the silent.

8.

Those who say 'No', are like a sabre

arriving on the frontlines a cold wind of death

and a deafening noise of shame,

those who stay become a knife

and to live on the edge of a knife

takes courage

or perhaps only pain.

9.

How can you not be afraid

that we'll all die, with this sound of hissing

that makes the long night unbearable?

How can you stand to be alone in such darkness

and not wonder if we could face

the night embracing each other,

the night like slime that covers our heads,

children on the damp sheets of a bed where

we would all suffocate at the same time?

PURGATORY

1.

You will trace new paths

without anger,

through the shrubs of holly, thorns and

branches that hamper our footsteps;

There will be no darkness anymore, despite

the whistling among the leaves

of birds of doom and the hoarse cries of fear.

But the dawn will be a skylark

with its long indifferent song,

rosy as the cheeks of children

in the winter light.

There will be no need anymore to act or to wait,

to oppose or to say "something,"

the words collapse

into the bitter interstices

the days will have their golden luster

without noise, a steady firmness

that makes even the silence beautiful.

That silence of

the countryside asleep in the sun,

no longer any omission or guilt

for not having spoken: instead there will be

a fire in which nothing burns, crying for rest.

But there is still the bitter loneliness

of defeat, the habit

that yesterday's knives tattooed on the skin

was almost like a boundary line.

And it seems just like yesterday, when you spoke: onward,

you must say it again and again.

Their voice is silent,

silent also is the hatred

that burned in you,

the fury.

But it's always the same, the desert,

and the road we walk with two directions.

There was only the wall,

the painted wooden wall.

But there are images

that they have always known,

inherent to the living, they said:

such as children laughing,

and the generations are not cumulative

they just follow one after the other.

And you did not possess the Book

only an ancient word

not a cry, like a lament

nor a vision that contained images

like those in the Book. And the others, tense mirrors

with clumsy but sure hands: down there no one knew the quickened

pulse in the wrist of the hand he uselessly attempted to hold –

in front of them,

was this the mistake? –

a mirror whose reflection

was exactly

the reflection of your face.

2.

A single tree

on the horizon,

a hanged man beneath

the expanse of clouds,

like a stake that splits the sky.

But the dry bushes blow

in front of the cloth.

Dark grass, a land

of crevasses, of fodder

and the foot stumbles everywhere

on the infested ground, of sorrow.

But this is your history

your times

and theirs never count.

Looking over your shoulder

you see all the filthy jealousies and grudges,

that shout, "Stay with us!"

and that cry out, "Bastard!"

You won't feel

any remorse

or fear.

The horizon, in front of you,

like something

you just typed in

and you knew

beforehand

that you were born of your mother's belly

and that she threw the baby away.

They still speak

those who can speak,

groaning and sighing below,

but they are the voices and faces of those inside,

sunk at the bottom but still leading,

hoarse masks of blackmail.

Don't look down,

tightrope walker!

Step

by step,

while down below,

they shout and try to make you fall,

into the mud

this region

filled with spiders and scorpions.

Step

by step,

even though they are at the bottom

they fake everything,

paradise and hell,

and their moans.

So pray then

with tears of parchment

to bruise the fragile rim of the eyes

but not even all that weeping

can force you

to look down

on those swarming faces

beaten by the gusts of wind:

now tears trailed after the mother

who swears loyalty;

now a cry for revenge;

now an order; it is the voice of the father

indistinguishable from the wind.

And your tears,

dark rain from this obscure point

in the sky, are your final

parting gift.

The dawn comes, rigid still

and now next to the profile of the mountains.

What remains after flight?

Hell or forgiveness?

You redden under the expanse

of cruel voices.

3.

And finally

here it is like a dream

without a landslide in time you find yourself

praying alone

just over the edge.

No god on the horizon,

but the faint shadow of a song

that welcomes you,

and warmth.

How much longer can you bear

this raising of sheets to the wind

and these sparkling meadows

this near awakening?

Ah, this is not a deception!

Dappled roadways and happy shadows,

green that descends gradually

towards an image of the lawn:

while inside

reality falls apart

and hisses

afraid of itself,

weakness that takes you from behind.

After a night like this

the walls are soaked with rain:

a quarter of light, a small quarter of light

and all the rest in shadow. But out of range,

and despite this, a strand of agony still

tears at the flesh.

And this light

was present just before the storm,

this clarity that spreads and consoles.

For an instant the universe

is absorbed into this spear of light

and in the silence perpetually active.

DRIFTING

There is a point at which the pain becomes audible: at first no, first

there is only the winter habit, where memories are durable fixtures.

Like signs. There is no difference between one direction or the other,

because of the cold and the bright white, a polished patina covering

the horizon. But there is a moment when suddenly an image is re-

covered from above, the path's crossroads and a seated child, crying.

From there begins a new concept of pain.

The gush of light in the morning has something icy about it, but

the stasis is perfect, genuine, let the baby cry. And why does he cry,

under that sun which cements his profile and holds him in anticipa-

tion, exhausted by the stings of the white?

He is discovering the plague

in the silence of the winds:

existence.

Inside the rotting meat of refusal,

the day makes you pay with your twisted nerves in a knot,

with red cervical bundles that are flammable,

the terms of laughter stored in the eyes.

A trap that jars,

his teeth sunk in the calf.

In the evening, already very late, here, during the winter,

there is a light that emerges from the depths,

a strip of white behind the buildings and the sky

a gray that fades into the blue that is frightening.

Gleam of anger,

behind the surface of a gaze,

the torn cloth of conscience.

Before nightfall,

and before continuing the bitter reality of the dream,

in this moment, in the final light and darkness,

there is a ceasefire and you are permitted to live.

Everything else is fleeing

and the night is sinking under sedation.

The body rebels against both evil and good,

the muscles contract and interweave the legs

and the voice at the bottom of the throat

(the contraction of two muscles

and the left vocal chord that refuses to stretch

and the other parts of you that protrude

as if you had silenced too many things

because the body doesn't rebel).

It's a trick of mirrors this sudden pain in the thigh:

the rebellion of the fibers,

the north wind that trembles

and the lowlands of the heart,

withered,

broken in so many places,

he's forgotten how to embrace himself.

Yet it is precisely this that yearns

to be accepted,

this black seed that is beautiful

inside his own will.

Like a chestnut hedgehog that yields to Autumn,

that surrenders itself.

BROTHERS II
(THE MEANING OF BATTLE)

What's different

about us,

brothers?

(Whom do we mean when we say *us*?)

I see the graves of silence

opened,

the regiment of deniers

take over the voice of the parade.

But the masks, oh what masks,

they are sewn right into the skin.

What need is there to shout, anymore,

pariahs?

When the mirror laughed in your face

there was no image that corresponded to you

without a sense of guilt. Brother.

And I know: they killed the one who shouted the loudest,

those crucified by the label,

whoever saluted the liberation

did it quickly,

before he was to be released

from inside.

But what else can we do?

Live with hate, contempt?

Live the quiet life?

What blush do you hide, brothers,

under the mask from your parade?

The first "We" raised.

We beat the kid on the inside

who didn't know that to join the march

the first thing he needed to do was scrub

his body for years and spend nights ridding himself of all the insults,

from that repository of voices: brothers sisters

legions of priests and moralists, doctors

and wise counselors.

The small wings of this first flight,

a deception that does not end

right up to the dawn of the telling.

How long will they look at us with contempt

and beat our heads against the wall

of this damp house, these uninhabitable houses?

To soar felt like

a cloud of abandonment,

night and misery

and shouting came from down below

where denial was the only word

they had taught us.

Because solitude was warm

like a hand, almost claw-like, in which to protect ourselves from the punch

that hit us right in the stomach and for days

left a taste of emptiness, a dark hunger.

Because solitude is an ocean

that sloshes around,

a labored awakening

was worth waiting for,

raising your eyes

was the greatest offense.

and the sharpest knife in the stomach.

There is exile only from yourself

and a private pain is a minor thing.

Alone, crying inside, is not

screaming along with everyone.

But if life has any meaning

then marching with anger beneath the windows

and with contempt for the past

is a way of saying

"We", "We, Everyone."

A Note by Pierre Lepori

This collection consists of two "books." *Whatever the name*, was composed prior to September 2000. It is a very personal attempt to come to terms with the silence and the waste of the familiar knot, to watch from the outside a case of emotional falsification stretched out over several generations. The goal – certainly too ambitious – had been to start medicating the language. This is the reason for certain purely descriptive inserts (though not devoid of affection), in a book born as a path towards the re-appropriation of language. The first section is proposed as a dialogue with the mother figure. The "Forms of Water" speaks of a physical experience: the dehydration of which I was a victim one month after birth, while I was at the mercy of a wet nurse. The Rimbaudian translation that closes the book is a sort of declaration of confidence in the word. I do not mean that it saves; only that it leads, as is always the case in poetry.

"Brothers" is instead an attempt to make political the detachment from the pain of silence. In the sections "Purgatory," "Pain," and "Drifting" I again gave free rein to a deeply personal anguish. But this second "book" should read like a journey, full of biographical themes, of course, but always looking for a responsible poetic language. A way out.

I would be ungrateful if I did not say that I had constant and very intense readings of these texts by Fabio Pusterla and Monique Laederach. Along with the vital closeness of Julien, and the nourishing friendships of Paola, Debora, Rita, and Natalia. Without their trust, I would never have dared to write.

PIERRE LEPORI was born in Lugano in 1968, studied in Siena and Bern (Dr. degree), and is now based in Lausanne (French-speaking Switzerland) . He is a writer and translator, and a journalist for the Swiss public radio network. He has translated French literature into Italian, including authors Monique Laederach, Gustave Roud, Claude Ponti. His literary works include: 'Qualunque sia il nome' (Schiller Prize for Poetry, 2004), 'Strade bianche' (2011), and three novels: 'Grisù' (2007), 'Sexualité' (2010) and 'Come cani' (published in Italian and French, with a self-translation). He's founder of Hétérographe, revue des homolittératures ou pas: "a queer literary review, and directs the Company " Théâtre Tome Trois" (TT3, Lausanne).

PETER VALENTE is the author of *A Boy Asleep Under the Sun: Versions of Sandro Penna* (Punctum Books, 2014),which was nominated for a Lambda award, *The Artaud Variations* (Spuyten Duyvil, 2014), *Let the Games Begin: Five Roman Writers* (Talisman House, 2015), a book of photography, *Street Level* (Spuyten Duyvil, 2016), and the chapbook, *Forge of Words a Forest* (Jensen Daniels, 1998). He is the co-translator of the chapbook, *Selected Late Letters of Antonin Artaud, 1945-1947* (Portable Press at Yo-Yo Labs, 2014), which includes six of Artaud's letters, and has translated the work of Luis Cernuda, Gérard de Nerval, Cesare Viviani, and Pier Paolo Pasolini, as well as numerous Ancient Greek and Latin authors. Forthcoming is a translation of Nanni Balestrini's *Blackout* (Commune Editions, 2017) and a book of photography, *Blue* (Spuyten Duyvil, 2017). His co-translation of 33 of Artaud's late letters with an introduction by Stephen Barber is forthcoming from City Lights. He is presently at work on a book for Semiotext(e). His poems, essays, and photographs have appeared or are forthcoming in journals such as *Mirage #4/ Periodical, First Intensity, Aufgabe, Talisman, Oyster Boy Review*, and *spoKe*. His work has also been published or is forthcoming online in *Talisman, The Poems and Poetics Blog, Oyster Boy Review, Jacket2, Sibilia, The Recluse, Dispatches From the Poetry Wars*, the *Verso Books blog*, and *Something on Paper*. In the late 1990s, he co-edited the poetry magazines *Vapor/Strains* and *Lady Blizzard's Batmobile* and wrote articles on jazz for the *Edgewater Reporter*. In 2010, he turned to filmmaking and has completed 60 shorts to date, 24 of which were screened at Anthology Film Archives.